The Annunaki Plan?

Or

The Human Plan?

One will kill You
the other
Will Save Your Life

Only You Can Choose

By
Chris Thoı

Fortynine Publishers

First Published in Great Britain in 2010
by
Fortynine Publishers

Chris Thomas asserts his right to be identified as the author of this book
in accordance with the Copyright, Designs and Patents Act, 1988.

A CIP catalogue record for this book
is available from the British Library

ISBN 978-0-9566696-0-5

Fortynine Publishers
PO Box 49
Llandysul
SA44 4YU

To order further copies of this book, please see the last page

Printed and bound in Wales by
Gomer Press, Llandysul, Ceredigion

1

Dedication

To

Di – Cariad Fi

and to

Eileen –
a constant supplier of friendship and support

Contents

Introduction

It would be fair to say that most people are aware that something is changing, this change occurring on every possible level of our existence. The problem is that there is a huge amount of misleading information and disinformation available, a great deal of which is deliberately intended to mislead us into making the wrong decision.

We are faced with a decision, one so fundamental to our existence that if we make the wrong one, individually and collectively, we place our existence on Earth in jeopardy. This might sound a little overly dramatic but it is becoming very clear that unless we make the right choice our lives will fall apart and we condemn the Earth to a very unstable future.

This choice is not about climate change, nor is it about pollution, nor is it about nuclear weapons but it is about our fundamental state of being, our very physical existence that is being put at risk.

This short book has been put together to try to help people understand what the options are and why these options are available to us at this particular time in our history and to place into its proper context the meaning of the date 2012.

This book is intended to be read by itself. However, it can also be read in conjunction with the author's nine other books on human history and development, particularly his most recent book (written with Dave Morgan), entitled *Project Human Extinction* and published in November 2009. This short book contains information that was not included in *Project Human Extinction* as well as new information that has come to light since. This book also pulls together several aspects of my previous books to highlight the conflict and the choice all of us are currently facing and to help to understand the choice we all have to make.

Much of the information within this book is highly secretive and controversial and those who are a part of the topic did not take my prying into the subject and their activities lightly. This has resulted in a number of attempts to take my life, over the past few years, some of which came close to being successful.

My history is that I began to wake up to there being something different going on in the world at about the age of seven. Like most children who show any psychic tendencies, the adults around me actively discouraged me from exploring this subject. Some years later, I realised that I had access to a source of information which was not usual and that I could provide answers to people on subjects of which I had no previous experience. I finally worked out that the source of information was the Akashic, the record keeping aspect of the human mass consciousness. About thirty years ago, I found that I could access the Akashic virtually at will; it was as though I was "hardwired" into it.

Also at this time in my life, I discovered that I was a natural healer. So for the past thirty years, I have been working as a healer, more recently in ways which are described as a psychic surgeon. I have also been investigating deeply into the Akashic to try to write the history of the human race, this is the truth of human history as recorded in the Akashic and not the propagandised version we indoctrinate our children with. I have written several books on human history and, with my wife Di, books on the true causes of illness and how healing actually works and, more importantly, how we can all cure ourselves of all ills without any form of medication or remedy.

I should say also that I do not work with guides or "entities" of any kind but access the Akashic directly through my higher self. This is not a form of channelling but more a process of obtaining knowledge directly from the source of that knowledge without any form of intermediary being.

For those who are unfamiliar with the Akashic, here's a brief description.

The term Akashic comes from ancient Sumeria, where their language was known as Sanskrit. The word Akashic is therefore a Sanskrit word which means "Record". This is a record of everything that happens on Earth, our solar system, our galaxy and, ultimately, the Universe as a whole. On Earth, we have developed a mass consciousness, what scientists would call a "morphic field". This mass consciousness records all of the events that take place on Earth and this mass consciousness then becomes part of the Akashic. The Akashic connects into the whole Universe in what quantum physicists are beginning to call the "Akashic Field". As the Akashic field connects in with the human mass consciousness, we can also download information from the rest of the Universe into our own level of understanding.

Many ancient, Eastern, traditions speak of the Akashic as the source of all ancient knowledge and wisdom, something scientists are finally beginning to accept.

Contained within the Akashic is the full record of every event that has ever occurred throughout the Universe since it first came into being.

The Akashic also contains a record of every event that has taken place on Earth. Although tracking through these records to follow the life of an individual is very difficult, it is possible to look back into history to find the truth of situations and events which have been distorted or propagandised by those with vested interests in presenting history to suit their own agendas.

We Are Not a Slave Race

The fundamental principle behind this book is to bring to light a version of human history that has gained popularity in the last few years – namely the story put forwards by a group of non-terrestrial beings who call themselves "Annunaki".

The Annunaki story states that they are the "creators" of mankind and their act of creation was to produce a race of slave peoples to serve their needs on Earth.

If we look around us at the way in which humanity has developed, especially since the start of the Industrial Revolution, we see that many people do believe that we are enslaved to corporations and the ideals presented by these corporations. It is not too huge a leap of the imagination to see how it is possible to make a connection between the concept of being a "wage slave" to accepting the huge mistruth that the Annunaki story could be true.

As we undergo our process of change, many are confused about who we are and why we are here and the Annunaki story of slave origins can seem attractive as it means that those who believe this fantasy do not have to take responsibility for bringing their own part of a process of completion to its conclusion but can rely on this non-terrestrial race to do everything for them.

In fact a large part of the "Annunaki Fantasy Story" is that they are here to take care of everything on our behalf and all we have to do is to step onto some kind of "space ship" which will whisk us away from Earth to a place where we can safely "ascend to the 5th dimension".

Many are falling for this alien propaganda and are undertaking meditations and other exercises intended to draw the Annunaki close to Earth. The eventual outcome of these beliefs and wishes is that humanity will not exist on Earth except for a small number, specified in the Annunaki Fantasy Story as being 500 million. These "chosen" 500 million will then be totally enslaved to the Annunaki.

What follows in this book is a précis of human history, as recorded in the Akashic, but with an emphasis on recent history, current events and the significance of the next two years leading up to the watershed date of 21st December 2012 (21/12/12).

There are many interpretations on the significance of this date and a number of them are misleading, some deliberately so. We also have propagandised movies, such as *"2012"*, attempting to tell us that this date is the end of all life and the planet. Then there is the Mayan Calendar which is also subject to a vast range of interpretations. The Mayan Calendar is one of many ancient calendar systems which all have in common an "end date" of 21/12/12.

The real significance of 2012 is that we come to the end of a cycle. It could be stated that this cycle began with the Creation of our Universe, or it began 85,000 years ago or even that it began 7,000 years ago – all of these dates are correct, it is the interpretation of these dates which has caused much of the current confusion.

Hopefully, by following the Akashic Records, I have been able to separate out the issues which are causing confusion and to place our future into its correct context.

As long as we make the correct choice, our future, and the future of the Earth, is assured for many thousands of years to come. If we make the wrong choice, succumb to the propaganda and lies, our future, and the future of the Earth, is very much in doubt.

Human History

This book is about human history, not as we currently understand it but in the way in which it is recorded within the Akashic. However, the events recorded within the Akashic are greatly at odds with the versions of human history we are used to hearing.

Really, there are four versions of human history: the scientific view, the creationist view, the Annunaki version and then the actual history as recorded within the Akashic.

The Annunaki version might be new to many people so I will be explaining about this a little later.

The Scientific View

To start with, let us begin with the one we are all familiar with – the scientific version. This is the history of human development as it is taught in schools and presented whenever the topic comes up for discussion.

According to paleoanthropologists, those scientists who dig up old bones and make up stories about them, claim that human life began in Africa.

According to this "official" version, the first pre-human being is called Australopithecus Afarensis. Australo meaning "southern", pithicus meaning "ape" and Afarensis is the Afar region of Africa where the bones were found. These remains are more commonly known as Lucy (these remains were called 'Lucy' as the paleoanthropologists who discovered them held a party that night to celebrate and the most popular piece of music played during the evening was the Beatles' song *"Lucy In The Sky With Diamonds"* so when they recovered from their hangovers the following morning, the remains were called Lucy and the name has stuck ever since).

After Lucy came Homo Erectus or "upright man", then Homo Habilis or "handy man", and then Cro-Magnon Man. Also, somewhere around here arrived Neanderthal Man. There have also been a number of other candidates for our first ancestor. For example, there was the 9 foot (3m) tall "Gigantopithicus", there was "Peking Man" and many others, most of them named for the region the remains were found in. Cro-Magnon Man then developed into our direct ancestors, Homo Sapien.

At some point, around 13,000 years ago, Lucy's descendents left Africa, in the middle of an Ice Age, and travelled north across Asia and Russia to cross the frozen Bering Sea and into Alaska where they then slowly travelled south until they reached South America. This whole process taking several hundred years to complete.

Think about that for a second; here you are living in your nice warm cave in a warm climate, you know where the water holes are and you know all of the game trails so you can feed yourself. So why would you leave all of that behind to trek thousands of miles across ice and frozen tundra? Especially as you did not know where you were headed for or what you were going to find along the way or even what you would find on arrival. If that was me, I'd have stayed in my nice warm cave and waited 'til spring.

All of this happening about 13,000 years ago. Remember this date of 13,000 years ago as it has significance in terms of where and how it originated. These travelling peoples are known as hunter gatherers or Homo Sapien – meaning "wise man". We have since evolved into Homo Sapien Sapien or wise, wise man – scientific arrogance at its best.

This is the "official" story of human development and woe betides anyone who contradicts it, especially anyone in a scientific or archaeological field.

Many scientific researchers have actually found themselves in the situation where they have uncovered human, or early human remains, which they have dated to times far earlier than 13,000 years ago and they have found themselves "drummed out" of their profession and not allowed to work in their scientific field again.

But if you investigate what is currently happening in archaeology and paleoanthropology you very quickly begin to realise that there is something not quite right in the official view. There are many failings in the scientific method, particularly in dating techniques but, what you do find in the archaeology of human remains is something very interesting, especially when modern DNA analysis techniques are used.

New DNA analysis of Lucy's remains show that the bones have no genetic connection to us but are, in fact, an early form of orang-utan. Homo Erectus and Homo Habilis are so similar, genetically, that they are the same. Neanderthal Man has no genetic connection to modern man and neither do the "false starts" like Gigantopithicus or Peking Man.

Our direct genetic ancestor is Cro-Magnon Man. What has been found is that wherever ancient early human bones are unearthed, the one finding that is consistent is that Cro-Magnon Man is found on every single continent, literally all over the world, and these early Cro-Magnon remains have been consistently dated as being three and a half million years old. This date of three and a half million years ago *does* have significance and I will come on to that later.

In other words, modern man did not originate in Africa but spontaneously appeared all over the world three and a half million years ago.

As these recent findings are totally at odds with the accepted, mainstream, scientific version of events, they are not made publicly known as the scientists insist on maintaining this myth of movement out of Africa thirteen thousand years ago. There is a reason for this and again I will come on to that later.

The Creationists' View

We will leave the scientific view for a moment and go on to the next version of human history which is the view of those who follow the Creationists' ideas.

Essentially, the Creationists' version of human history follows the story given in the Old Testament. In other words, "God" created the Earth in six days and then created Adam followed by Eve and

13

they lived in the Garden of Eden. Eve then persuaded Adam to eat of the fruit of the tree of knowledge and they were evicted from Eden. Once outside of the Garden of Eden, these two first humans got to "know" each other, in the Biblical sense, and the rest of the human race followed.

But God doesn't leave it there, he takes pity on his creations and directs their lives on an almost day to day basis to try and keep us on the straight and narrow.

There is a reason why this version of history arose and, believe it or not, this reason connects the Creationists' view and the scientific view together and that explanation is tied into the third version of human history.

The Annunaki Plan

To understand this third version, we have to think a little seriously about our Universe. Does anybody still seriously think that we are alone in this Universe? Would a Universe of the immensity of ours only exit for the sole benefit of life on Earth? Cosmologists have recently discovered thousands of Earth-like planets within our galaxy alone; surely some of them must be inhabited. The reality is that there are thirteen other races out there, most of whom have had some kind of direct contact with the Earth and I will explain the information contained within the Akashic, about these races, a little later.

Even the Vatican has made several statements, over the past few years, stating that they accept, and believe in, the existence of human-like races other than those to be found on Earth (there are a number of books reporting these statements, one such book being *Hidden Truth Forbidden Knowledge* by Dr Steven Greer).

This next version of human history has been written by one of these races for reasons that are not beneficial to humans.

This third version of our history has been devised by beings that are not of this Earth, not even of our galaxy. This version has been formulated by a group of beings known as the Annunaki. Not only have the Annunaki made this story up but they have also been promoting it by persuading politicians and world leaders, but in particular those who have the control over governments, that this plan is the way in which humanity was created and how we should progress.

This plan has been at work for approximately 5,000 years and its ultimate aim is to reduce the human population to around about 500 million worldwide. In other words, the population of the whole world would reduce from the current official count of 6.9 billion down to only 500 million (a reduction of six thousand four hundred million). This reduction can not happen naturally. The

500 million that remain would become a "slave race" to the Annunaki.

This third version of human history I will call The Annunaki Plan. This plan works in two ways, both of which attacks and tries to force humans to forget The Human Plan, the real and fourth story of human history, and follow the Annunaki Plan instead. This is its purpose. It might sound melodramatic or like the plot from a second-rate science fiction movie but it is happening and the biggest problem of all is that those who are in a position of power on Earth believe in this plan and are enforcing it upon the rest of the human population. This plan is also designed to come to fruition in 2012.

So what is this plan?

Really it is a story that tries to hide our true history and impose a different version of the development of human life on Earth. The problem is that many thousands of ordinary people, worldwide, are falling for this plan without realising its implications and are welcoming in the Annunaki. All of the recent requests for groups to meditate on a particular theme because it "helps the planet" or helps humans to "ascend" to a "fifth dimension", have been designed to help the Annunaki to fulfil this plan of theirs and are of no benefit to the Earth at all or to humans.

An example of this would be the mass meditation to "Fire up the Grid" (in August 2007) or the attempt at taking over the energy point under Silbury Hill in Wiltshire (on 7th August 2009) or the call for a mass meditation to "energise the crystal deposits under Brazil and Arizona" (on 15th-20th August 2009). All of these meditations were designed to fool people into believing that they were helping the Earth whereas what they were really doing was furthering the plans of the Annunaki or the Hathor and causing problems for the Earth and humanity – I'll come back to this.

The Annunaki Fantasy Story

Here is the Annunaki fantasy story. This is based on translations made by Zecharia Sitchin and published in his many books on the subject.

The story is imprinted into clay tablets that have been found buried in the sands of ancient Sumeria that have lain there for over 5,000 years. Zecharia Sitchin is an expert on Sumerian cuneiform writing and it is he who has translated these clay tablets into English over the past 40 years. Zecharia Sitchin did not make this story up, what he has done is to translate ancient clay tablets and bring the story to light.

The story begins some time in the past when a new planet enters our solar system. This planet orbits at an angle to and in the opposite direction of the rest of the planets and has the name of Nibiru. Nibiru has an orbit that takes 3,600 years to complete, passing through our solar system and travelling out far into space before returning. On two of its orbits, it created a great deal of damage to the existing planets in our solar system and was responsible for creating our Earth by splitting another planet into two halves; one half forming the Earth, the other half of this destroyed planet forming the asteroid belts.

I am only going to give a brief description here, if you want more detail you will have to read the books by Zecharia Sitchin - they make a fascinating read (see Bibliography).

Following this disaster, the solar system finally settled down with Nibiru as a permanent member of the solar system but still only visiting us every 3,600 years.

The inhabitants of Nibiru are the Annunaki. Their planet, travelling through deep space, eventually causes problems within Nibiru's atmosphere and, after a period of study, the Annunaki come to the conclusion that to repair their atmosphere, they need to seed it with gold. They studied all of the planets within our solar system and discovered that the planet with the greatest amount of gold deposits is Earth so a plan is made whereby a party of

Annunaki will travel to Earth and extract the necessary gold from seawater.

The individual placed in charge of the whole operation is called Enlil with an individual called Enki in a kind of chief engineer's role. Both travel to Earth, together with a number of Annunaki who were to carry out the gold extraction from the sea, specifically the Red Sea and the North Africa coast. The party arrives about 450,000 years ago setting up their main encampment in the region of Sumeria – between the Tigris and Euphrates rivers, a region they name Eden.

Everything goes well to start with but they cannot extract sufficient quantities of gold from the sea so they switch their centre of operations to land and they begin to excavate gold mines in Africa.

Although they begin gold mining in Africa, their main centre of operations remains in Eden in Sumeria. Eventually, Enlil leaves the planet leaving Enki in full control. As gold is mined, it is stockpiled until the next orbit of Nibiru brings it closer to Earth where the gold is then ferried back to their home world.

After a while, the Annunaki who are carrying out the mining work, begin to complain that it is much harder work than they signed on for, putting the whole operation at risk. Enki comes up with an idea and that is to genetically modify the proto-humans (probably Homo Erectus/Habilis) that are on the planet to make them more intelligent and able to carry out the hard work of mining.

The Annunaki have a technology that uses genetic engineering that they developed a very long time ago. This is a technology based on the use of something like a "computer master disc" called a Me (pronounced May) which is capable of managing immensely complex processes such as genetic manipulation and it is this technology which Enki puts to use to create a new slave race.

Following a great deal of trial and error, Enki succeeds in producing an Annunaki/Homo Erectus hybrid. In other words, the genetic structure of the Annunaki is mixed with the genetic structure of Homo Erectus to create a new type of human being. This new hybrid Enki calls "adamu".

18

At first, the adamu are unable to reproduce by themselves and so are born to Annunaki females. Again, they become tired of this, especially as there are an insufficient number of adamu to mine the gold in sufficient quantities. So Enki then sets to work again to make his adamu capable of sexual reproduction. In other words, Enki "creates" adamu in Eden but then further creates a female adamu (Eve, presumably) to allow the adamu to self-replicate. This now works extremely well, the adamu are reasonably intelligent and they work hard. They also begin to replicate in large numbers and the Annunaki train them to grow crops. The adamu are short and dark whilst the Annunaki represent themselves as tall and pale. The main symbol adopted by the Annunaki is the "winged disc" – a central disc with eagle's wings on either side – a symbol also found in dynastic Egypt. I'll come back to the reason for this symbol a little later.

At this point, a problem begins to build. The Annunaki find the adamu females very attractive and begin to mate with them. This produces another hybrid form, with a much paler skin than the adamu. These hybrids begin to demand that they have equal rights to the Annunaki themselves, after all, the Annunaki tradition is that the rights of inheritance passes through the male line and as the new hybrids have Annunaki fathers, they should have equal rights to the Annunaki who fathered them. This leads to a great upheaval within the Annunaki and Enlil is forced to return to Earth to rule on this problem of inheritance. Some of the new hybrids are accepted whilst others are not but, the final outcome is that Enlil orders that the adamu be allowed to die. In response, the Annunaki remove all support, food, medicine, etc for the adamu and, effectively leave them to die. However, the adamu prove to be extremely resilient and survive.

It was then noticed that the next orbit of Nibiru will bring it close to the South Pole which will have the effect of melting all of the ice causing a flooding of most of the Earth's surface together with major earthquakes and volcanoes. Enlil orders Enki to evacuate the Annunaki off the planet's surface and further orders him to not inform the adamu of their fate. However, Enki is very fond of his creations and secretly helps an adamu, called Utnapishtim (the Biblical Noah), to build an Ark to save as many of the adamu as possible as well as all types of animals and plants.

The Ark is actually a submarine boat and, instead of the animals "going in two by two", Utnapishtim has Me's which contain the genetic records of all life.

With the next orbit of Nibiru, the anticipated disruption begins and massive floods occur which also end the last Ice Age. This all taking place about 13,000 years ago.

Remember I asked you earlier to take note of this date of 13,000 years ago because it is all tied up with this Annunaki story. As this happened 13,000 years ago, the scientific theories were built around it regardless of the evidence contradicting them and why the scientists stick to their story that humans first developed in Africa.

Anyway, the flood waters finally recede and Enlil, Enki and the remainder of the Annunaki return to Earth. At first, Enlil is extremely angry that Enki disobeyed his orders but, eventually, he begins to realise that Enki was right to do so as the adamu prove to be very useful as a slave race.

The Annunaki set about repairing their infrastructure in Sumeria, or Eden, and decide to step up their gold mining operation as well as to establish a "way-station" on Mars. The Mars way-station is decided upon as Nibiru's future orbits will take it closer to Mars than to the Earth and so it will be easier and more efficient to ferry the mined gold to Mars and then on to Nibiru as its orbits allow. In order to help in this increase in flight traffic they build "flight beacons" and flight control stations next to the River Nile – the Pyramids.

At this point, the story told in Zecharia Sitchin's translations gradually begins to tail off and does not come to any conclusions.

So, what does this story actually tell us? Well, it says that humans were created by the Annunaki to be a slave race – the adamu. The adamu are short, with black skin and originate in Eden – modern day Iran and Iraq - but develop in Africa. The Annunaki, in Sitchin's translations, describe themselves as being "tall and blond" – "Tall White Nordics" it would appear. The adamu thrive and multiply and travel to other regions of the Earth at the end of the last Ice Age, or just after, around about 13,000 years ago. Up until this point, the adamu had been restricted to regions of Africa where the Annunaki were mining gold. There were also new hybrid adamu created by the Annunaki mating with adamu females presumably producing children with a skin colour much closer to that of the Annunaki - in other words, white.

Zecharia Sitchin insists that this story is the basis for the Biblical Old Testament.

Unfortunately, some people believe that they are the direct descendents of the Annunaki/adamu hybrids and these people see themselves as being a more elite group than the rest of humanity, who they see as being descended from the adamu. After all, if you are made "in God's image", you must be special and, therefore, above all other humans. This "elite" group has also given rise to racism and the concept of white supremacy. This elite group are the ones who make up the Illuminati, Bilderburgers and the Thirtieth level Freemasons and allied groups.

It has to be borne in mind that there is nothing within the Akashic that agrees with this story. However, there are some clues as to how aspects of this story arose which were then manipulated by the Annunaki to give us their fictitious version.

The Basis of the Annunaki Story

Firstly, are there any Earthly traditions to support the idea of "tall white" beings mating with early humans? The answer is yes, there are and they are centred around the Tigris and Euphrates Rivers, particularly modern northern Iraq, southern Turkey and Turkistan (backed up by recent archaeological findings at Gobekli Tepe).
There are a collection of beliefs which originate from this area, generally known as the "Cult of Angels".

The main traditions of these cults are that the people living in this area called it Eden. The peoples are hunter gatherers who are invaded by a group of peoples who originate much further north. These northern invaders are much taller than the locals and are possibly albino, but certainly pale skinned – the origin of "tall white Nordics" perhaps. These tall northerners could also be a now defunct hereditary line from Gigantopithicus. The original peoples call these northern interlopers "Nephilim". The Nephilim have almond shaped eyes which slope in towards the nose giving their skulls a "bird-like" appearance. These northerners also have traditions connected with birds, using bird feathers and bird wings in rituals. They also practiced human sacrifice. One of the main symbols connected with this "Cult of Angels" is the winged disc.

These white northerners are very aggressive and very charismatic, so much so that they treat the local inhabitants as slaves and take to themselves a god-like status. They mated with the local women and produced hybrid children, known as "children of the jars". In order to feed their "gods", the peoples are forced into leaving behind their traditional hunter-gatherer way of life and become farmers.
Also in this region is the ancient Biblical city of Ur of the Chaldes where Abraham was born; Abraham being the "father" of the three main religions – Judaism, Islam and Christianity, but was also a member of the "Cult of Angels".

The eventual outcome is that having put up with these aggressive northerners for some time, they massacre them, totally destroying all of their kind.

Eventually, these peoples moved south from northern Iraq, or put another way, were cast out of Eden, and they moved to Egypt, taking these traditions and symbols with them with the white northerners transposed into their vengeful Gods. These members of the "Cult of Angels" eventually left Egypt led by Moses, the Egyptian Pharaoh Akhenaton the third, and became the Jewish peoples with their traditional stories forming the basis of the Old Testament.

It is these cultural memories and traditions which the Annunaki have taken and modified to form the basis of their adamu story.

Secondly, is there any evidence whatsoever of a travelling planet which orbits our sun, passing in and out of our solar system whether called Nibiru or by any other name?

According to the accepted archaeological view, virtually every single ancient site, from the Stone Age onwards, was used as some kind of astronomical observatory. This means that humans have watched the skies for many thousands of years.

It is known that the ancient Sumerians and the ancient peoples of South America used telescopes with evidence pointing to their use over 18,000 years ago. The Chinese have been keeping very accurate star charts and details of planetary movements for at least 5,000 years. Celtic, Egyptian, Tibetan, Native North American, Inuit, African and Australian Aboriginal civilisations were all known to observe the skies with great accuracy, so much so that many ancient beliefs concerning the stars and star systems were not confirmed until very recently, some requiring the observational power of the Hubble Space Telescope before the ancient knowledge was believed by scientists.

Do any of these traditions have any records of a travelling planet – no. Do any of these traditions have any records of a planet

23

appearing and disappearing every 3,600 years – no. So the actual existence of Nibiru, and therefore the Annunaki, is not recorded anywhere in Earth traditions. If Zecharia Sitchin's translations of orbit times and planetary appearances are in any way accurate, then the last time that Nibiru passed close to the Earth was about 2,200 years ago. Are there any records of a new planet entering our solar system at this time? – no. So as far as our historical records are concerned, there is no evidence of Nibiru's existence at all.

But, does the Akashic record any planets with the name Nibiru? Yes, there is a planet called Nibiru that is inhabited by a race who call themselves Annunaki but they are nowhere near to our solar system, in fact they are not even of our galaxy but are in a galaxy 23 galaxies away from ours behind the constellation of Sagittarius.

The Akashic's View of the Annunaki.

The Annunaki originate in a solar system that has two suns, around these two suns orbit eight planets; three planets orbit one sun whilst four orbit around the other; the eighth planet orbits around both suns, taking the equivalent of 3,600 Earth years to do so. This eighth planet is known to its inhabitants as Anu as well as Nibiru.

This is obviously where the Annunaki originate although their solar system is known as Velus, after the primary solar system consciousness, and the inhabitants of the solar system are known as Velon. The Velon peoples are semi-physical in energy patterns (see later for an explanation) and so are much less physically dense than we are. Although collectively they are known as Velon, they have divided themselves into six different races. These racial differences are difficult to describe in human terms but seem to follow some kind of "religious" division. These six "races" are: Johnaan, Oa, Mila, Jjundaa, Hathor, and Annunaki. These divisions are a little like countries on Earth. We do not call ourselves "earthlings" or even humans very often but prefer Italian, Australian, Russian, etc. Another analogy would be people on

24

Earth being known by their religious beliefs; Jewish, Christian, Islamic, Buddhist etc. It is the same with the Velon.

Most of the population live on the main planet called Velus but also inhabit several of the other planets as well having a technology which allows them to travel freely throughout their galaxy.

Some time ago, a disaster happened in the Velus system where one of the planetary moons collided with one of the planets (see my previous books for full details) causing a great deal of destruction and the population of that planet moved to other planets in the Velus system to avoid the catastrophe.

The home world of the Annunaki, called either Anu or Nibiru, has an atmosphere which contains very dense particles in order to keep the surface habitable as the planet travels the vast distances as it orbits around both suns. The nearest description of what this dense substance is made from would be gold dust.

As far as the solar system itself is concerned, the primary solar system consciousness, Velus, appears to have lost interest in its solar system as the suns are slowly dying.

The Velon are a peoples who have kept themselves very much to themselves with very little contact with any of the other ET races. In fact, they seem to have remained primarily within their home galaxy. However, about 1,000 years ago one of the Velon ships broke through the energy boundary of their home galaxy and discovered an energy flow.

Throughout this universe, there are always free moving energies. Some of these energy flows are targeted at specific regions to, say, help in that region's development. Unfortunately, for us, the energy flow detected by the Velon ship was the primary energy flow directed at our solar system (this energy is intended to help us in our experiment on Earth and is directed at Silbury Hill in Wiltshire). The reporting of this energy flow caused a massive revelation within the Velus system and sparked a race to try to be the first of the six Velon races to arrive at the end of this energy flow. The Velus consciousness seems to have had some kind of strange "religious" moment at this news and began to see the Velon as "God's chosen people" who should live on "God's chosen planet", in other words, the Velon should move to Earth.

The first Velon ships to arrive at our solar system did so about 300 years ago. On seeing that the Earth was inhabited, they decided to observe rather than to land – had they landed on Earth at that time, humanity's chances of still being on Earth now would have been very slim.

Again, there is a great deal more detail available than I have space for here (see my other books if you require more information), however several things did happen. The majority of the Velon races decided that they did not want to supplant another peoples and so they went to a new solar system, leaving what could be called "the conquest of the Earth" to the most aggressive of the Velon – the Annunaki and the Hathor.

What must be remembered is that these two groups were in competition with each other with the prize being the domination of the Earth. To achieve these aims the two groups took two different courses of action. The Hathor by approaching people through channelled means – they were very successful at this and persuaded one large group in America to sow the seeds of humanity's destruction for themselves by building two devices called "cellestoriums". These were copper lined shafts 333 feet (100 metres) deep which were packed with programmed quartz crystals – essentially, they acted like giant tuning forks buried vertically into the ground. These devices were designed to draw the souls out of the body and eject it to the now empty Velus solar system. The first of these two devices was activated on the 10th April 2006 and those who were a part of this group felt the full effects of this device. Fortunately, those who act as guardians of this Earth arrived in time to stop this mass murder from taking place. Had both devices been activated at the same time, everyone on Earth would have been affected, to one degree or another.

These two "tuning forks" were also designed to have a major impact on the Earth's own frequencies and two of the Sidhé were destroyed when the first cellestorium was activated. No Sidhé have ever been destroyed before this event.

The Hathor have been, generally speaking, very quiet since although they have been channelling music sequences to people on Earth with the hope that the music will have the same affect as the cellestoriums.

The Annunaki, however, took a different approach. The Annunaki had studied the Earth, and humanity, in great detail and had gained an in-depth knowledge of how we thought and how we acted. This was mainly achieved by implanting energy devices into peoples' bodies without their consent. These implants acted a little like cameras and sound recorders which transmitted back to the Annunaki every event that took place in these peoples' lives. These transmissions were made in real time so every aspect of life was sent back to the Annunaki as they happened 24 hours a day, 365 days a year, all of this happening without those who had been implanted with these devices knowing that their lives were being minutely monitored and transmitted in this way.

The Annunaki saw our religious beliefs and decided to put together a story which blended together the history of their solar system and some of our basic beliefs. What they finally came up with is the story we very briefly outlined earlier. In other words, the Annunaki story is a complete fabrication designed very deliberately to make humanity believe that the Annunaki are the "gods" of the Old Testament and that they, the Annunaki, are our creators. The story also made us a slave race and so they hoped that if we fully accepted the story, when they made themselves known on Earth in the present time, we would automatically see them as our "gods" and do whatever it was they instructed us to do as their slaves.

This is not to say that I think Zecharia Sitchin is complicit in the Annunaki plan. I believe him to be totally innocent in this. What Sitchin has done is to take a collection of clay tablets that are covered in cuneiform writing and translate them. His translations have brought the Annunaki story to light. What Sitchin has done is to honestly translate the writing on clay tablets that have been buried under the sands of what was ancient Sumeria for over 5,000 years. The reason why the story and the tablets, have been buried away for 5,000 years is that the Annunaki travelled back in time to deliberately plant their story.

I am not going into the rights and wrongs of the concept of time travel here, but the reason the Annunaki chose Sumeria 5,000 years ago is very specific.

I will explain this a little more fully when we get to the true history of the Earth, but, essentially the region known as southern Sumeria is where a peoples lived who explored human life in what could be described as "scientific" ways. It was the southern Sumerians who developed medicine, surgery, herbalism, aromatherapy, Ayurveda, and a whole lot of other ways of working with the body. All of this information was originally communicated psychically but, by about 7,000 years ago, we had generally lost these psychic capabilities and the Sumerians began to develop a written form of language which archaeologists call "cuneiform". This is why the Annunaki chose to travel back to this time; this was the first time that written records began to be kept.

When they travelled back in time, the Annunaki had taken with them their, to us, very advanced technology. To meet their energy needs they used what they called "djed pillars". These are virtually inexhaustible crystal-based energy sources which have the energy capacity equivalent to several power stations; they also took their Me technology with them.

This story was dictated to a Sumerian scribe and, shortly after the story was recorded, the people of Sumeria began to migrate to other lands; the northern Sumerians to Egypt and the southern Sumerians through Babylon, then India and finally settled in Tibet. The Annunaki, who were in southern Sumeria, decided to travel with the southern Sumerians and they also took up residence in Tibet, where they remained until fairly recent times.

The Annunaki have a problem living amongst humans because of their appearance. The Velon vary between 8 and 15 feet in height (2.4 to 4.5 metres), depending on which one of the six races they are, with their heads, proportionately, being very small. Given this appearance, they could not mix amongst humans and took to hiding. However, during this time, they did begin experimenting with their Me technology to try to genetically alter their appearance so that they looked more like humans. This Me technology allows them to fully detach the soul from the body and reside within the Me, the Me then builds a new body from scratch. Once the new body form is complete, the soul is then slowly downloaded from the Me into the new body.

Following experiments covering several thousand years, they perfected a body type that is almost identical to a human body but is pure Velon. Very few of these Annunaki humans exist.

So, the Annunaki kept watch on human development and human actions and aspirations. When they felt the time was right, they began their move to control the future of humanity. This was in 1776 when the international banker, Amschel Rothschild, decided to bring together 12 of his most trusted friends and colleagues to form the Bavarian Illuminati.

The Annunaki moved very quickly into control of this group and have been in control of them ever since. The first thing the Illuminati did was to take control of the Freemasons as the Freemasons had access to secret information that related to the Human Plan and other related matters of human history.

Next, the Illuminati re-formed the Knights Templar (the Knights having been destroyed by the Vatican and the French King in 1307) because of their original role in safeguarding the Ark of the Covenant and the knowledge it contained – the Tables of Testimony. These Tables of Testimony were actually a green crystal which had been programmed with the whole of human history and so showed the Annunaki story as a lie. The Annunaki do not control the Ark and so have not been able to destroy the crystal.

With the Freemasons and the Knights Templar firmly under Illuminati and Annunaki control, they began to look for ways of flexing their muscle and begin the process of building A New World Order.

Hopefully you can begin to see how the Creationery version of human history and the scientific version have originated. The Annunaki story has formed the belief that Adam (or adamu) and Eve were created as the first humans in the Garden of Eden but were to populate the Earth after the Flood 13,000 years ago. The scientific version of human history also ties in with the Annunaki story in that the first humans appeared in Africa and began to migrate around the world about 13,000 years ago.

The Akashic's Version of Human History

These three versions of human history, outlined above, are false in that they do not reflect the real breadth of humanity, our experiences or our potential. To find out the real history of humanity, we need to turn to our collective mass consciousness, the Akashic. This true version of human history the Akashic records as "The Human Plan".

Some people will find much of what follows to be a little weird, especially if they have not before considered other forms of life throughout the Universe. Whilst for others, it will fill in the gaps to explain what is really going on.

To understand ourselves, and our place within the Universe, as well as our place on Earth, we have to return to the beginnings of the Universe and the purpose of its Creation. This information is taken from the Akashic but backed up by "physical" research where that research is available. To give a full history is obviously not possible in the space we have available. I used to give one day workshops, seven hours of talking, and, even then, we would run out of time. So this can only be a very brief view of history - if you require a fuller version, all I can suggest is that you read my books.

For once, science has gotten one thing exactly right and that is the age of the Universe - 14.5 billion years old. It did not just spontaneously spring into being but was created by a being that encompasses all of the energy available everywhere. This Creationery source had a thought, a kind of "what would happen if..." For our Universe, the thought was Freedom of Choice. That is, each soul that was to be created to explore this Thought has the absolute right to choose their actions and their place within this Universe. The only "Law" that applies to this Universe is that no one can act in such a way as to remove someone else's freedom to choose their own actions.

There are other universes but the others explore different thoughts, other ways of being and, really speaking, these other universes do not have a bearing on our universe and so, for all practical purposes, they can be ignored. These are "real" universes in the same way as our universe is real. These are not the "multiverses" of quantum theory.

There are two points to remember here. The first is that everything is energy. What looks and feels solid to us is, in fact, a collection of energy frequencies which our brains "see" as being physical but is in fact compacted and compressed frequencies of energy.

The other point is that every living thing is a consciousness, a soul. From the universe itself, the galaxies, solar systems, stars, planets, animals and plants, all are souls. Some exist as a whole soul, some as part of another soul and some as group souls. Nevertheless, all is consciousness and all is energy. That is how our universe is constructed and how it works – souls using their potential to make use of the energies that are available to them. I see the words soul and consciousness as being interchangeable, so if I sometimes use the word soul or sometimes use the word consciousness, they both mean the same thing.

So, fourteen and a half thousand million years ago, this Creationery source had a Thought and this Thought was brought into being by creating a balloon of energy – the universal envelope – into which all of the energy frequencies necessary for life and exploration of the Thought was placed. At each stage of development other energies were added as necessary until we have the universe we are familiar with today.

This originating Thought could also be described as a Question – a "what would happen if..."?

In order to explore the Creator's Question, individual souls were created and provided with enough energy potential to fulfil their chosen role.

The first souls were thirteen beings who, effectively, make up the universal envelope. These Thirteen maintain the balance of energies within the universe and act as co-creators as and when necessary.

The next level of development was the creation of those souls who would bring galaxies into being. These were followed by souls who could build solar systems and then all of the way down to souls, consciousnesses, who would build individual planets.

Once these consciousnesses were in place, the first free-moving and free-acting souls were brought into creation. These first beings entered into our universe 100 million years ago. There are six of these first races who are of pure soul energy. In other words, they have a form, an outline, which is human in shape but they do not have any physical density, just pure energy. In Biblical terms, these beings could be described as "Angels". These six non-physical races are where the souls of virtually all humans originate – almost everyone is a "closet Angel"! In this sense there are no "old souls" or "new souls", the vast majority of souls on Earth are 100 million years old. What makes people appear to be old or new souls is their level of understanding of life.

The next stage of development took place about 30 million years ago with the Creation of seven semi-physical races. These are the races that are responsible for UFO sightings over the years. By semi-physical, I mean that they have a physical form and a physical density and, to each other, they appear as solid as we do to each other. However, if you had one of these beings standing in front of you now, the chances are that you would not even know that they were there, unless you were very psychic. The reason for this is that they are constructed of energy frequencies that are outside of the ability of human senses to detect.

There are seven of these semi-physical races, each having their own characteristics and each having their own region of the universe to live in, usually encompassing several galaxies. Some of these races we have names for such as Sirians or Pleiadeans whilst others we have only star chart references for, such as NGC 584 whilst others we only have nick-names for such as the infamous Greys or the Blues.

Generally speaking, all of these races are benevolent and have been helpful to the Earth and to us over many thousands of years. The only exception is the Velon we spoke about earlier.

So these are the thirteen races that make up the free-moving, free-acting and free-choosing souls who inhabit this universe. Each of these races is made up of many billions of souls. The six non-physical races can move freely throughout the whole of the universe without the need for any form of craft to travel. They just think themselves where they want to go and they just travel along the thought. The seven semi-physical races do need craft and these are the UFO's or NTV's – Non-Terrestrial Vehicles, as they are now called. These semi-physical races have also spread out from their original home worlds and live on many planets in different galaxies.

To avoid confusion, when I talk of these races, I talk of soul-origin. What I mean by this is, I often get people coming up to me and saying that they have had past-life regression or they have been told by a medium or clairvoyant that they come from – let's say – the planet "Zog". That may well be true, they may very well be a "Zoglith" but, their soul origin might be Pleiadean or Sirian or any of the seven semi-physical races.

To give you an example. Some years ago, people were contacted by a race who called themselves Oomite. They were very polite beings who contacted people by very politely written letters. Now they were correct in calling themselves Oomites as that was their home planet but, their soul origin is Pleiadean.

The Development of Our Solar System

Now we come to the development of life on Earth.

Our solar system is unique. It was designed to be a place where another aspect of the Question asked by the Creator could be explored – is life at the energy densities that we consider "physical" possible? In order to explore this aspect of the "Question", our solar system was planned to be, essentially, self-contained. Our solar system is also positioned at the back end of nowhere. This was also quite deliberate as we could explore all of the aspects we wished to explore but also be separate from the ebb and flow of universal energies and universal life.

Our solar system is also unique in the sense that each of the planets is an individual soul. In virtually all other solar systems, the sun is the primary consciousness and any planets are a part of that sun's consciousness. In other words, in those solar systems, the sun and planets are one soul. In our solar system, because we were to be a new experiment in life, it was decided that each of the planets, as well as the sun, needed to have as full a potential for life as possible and so the sun and each planet are individual souls.

Our solar system began to form about 40 million years ago. I appreciate that 40 million years is nowhere near the 4 billion, or so, years that cosmologists talk about, but 40 million years is what the Akashic records.

There were originally 13 planets in our system, each developing life in the way in which that planet's consciousness decided to create life. Each of our planets is a creator in its own right, this is why a full consciousness was needed for each planet, to maximise potential and creativity. Every single one of these 13 planets developed their own forms of life, all of which were what we would term physical.

Each individual planet designed and created forms of life which it felt was appropriate to its own consciousness. This provided for the maximum amount of creativity and diversity and all were successful. Each planet supported life and the Universe gloried in the complexity and variations in form.

Our Earth was a slightly late starter in this process as She did not begin to fully develop life until about 25 million years ago. This date of 25 million years is actually borne out by early scientific investigation into the development of life on Earth.

The 25 million year period was widely accepted by biologists and zoologists until geologists became involved and tried to fit the 25 million years into their theories of how rocks are formed. Given the geologists' theories required increasingly longer periods of time for sedimentation to occur as well as the formation of other types of rock, the age of the Earth was made progressively longer and longer, regardless of the evidence to the contrary. The current scientifically accepted date of 4 billion years was arrived at by dating the age of a meteorite. Nobody knows where this meteorite originated but it is assumed that as everything was formed at the same time following The Big Bang (see later), everything in the Universe must be the same age and so it makes no difference that this meteorite is not an Earth rock, it just needs to be a rock that fits into their theories and gives the scientists a date they can work with.

Regardless of any dates, the Earth was as successful as all of the other planets in the solar system in developing a huge range of life-forms. The Earth began with the extremely small, making use of many of the organisms that exist within the Universe, but very rapidly moved to big – as in the dinosaurs, giant trees and giant insects. The reason for this was to do with the effects of physical density on the physical body, once it was realised that smaller forms of life were just as feasible as the large, mammals became the primary forms of life and the plant-life was redesigned and created to suit the needs of these kinds of animals.

The scientific view is that there have been a series of ice ages or natural disasters which wiped out all life and then new life began to develop after these disasters. This is not true, apart from one major catastrophe, the forms of life, and the changes that have taken place to them, have all occurred because of a deliberate choice of the Earth's consciousness – a kind of fine tuning of design or the realisation that some life-forms were not fully viable and needed to be changed for new designs. In other words, all of the animal and plant life on Earth has been designed and created or adopted by the Earth herself. With a Universe of free choice, why would the Creator impose It's view on anything?

About 3.9 million years ago, four of the planetary consciousnesses, within our solar system, decided that they did not want to remain a part of this solar system and chose to leave. Unfortunately, in removing themselves from their planetary shells, they triggered a solar system-wide disaster which virtually destroyed all life in the solar system.

The first two planets to leave did so quite rapidly and the planets, the planetary consciousness had built around themselves, for want of a better word, exploded. One of these planets was positioned between Venus and Earth and the other between Mars and Jupiter. The resulting explosions created a wave of destruction throughout the whole solar system. Virtually all solar system life was destroyed. Only two planets still supported life: Earth and Ganymede, one of the Moons of Jupiter. Virtually all of the life on Earth was destroyed, the planet was rocked on its equatorial axis and a large quantity of the atmosphere was lost. Life on Earth was almost abandoned because of this disaster but the Earth decided to start again. Apart from Ganymede, all of the other planets decided to think again and did not begin rebuilding life until very recently – more about this later.

It is this solar system-wide disaster which the Annunaki decided to use as the background for their fantasy story but blending it with events that took place within their own solar system.

The debris from these 'exploding' planets formed the asteroid belts and several planets, including Earth, gained a moon. The other two planets, who had decided to leave, did so much more

37

gently, moving the whole planet to a position just inside of the solar system's limits. The location and gravitational influence of these two planets on Pluto and Uranus has given rise to speculation, in recent years, of a tenth planet – Planet X.

Three million, six hundred thousand years ago, the Earth began again but, this time, She was not beginning from scratch.

The primary purpose of the Earth, and our solar system, was to explore the possibility of "physical" life, that is, a physical body which was capable of containing a whole soul. Each of the planets, throughout the solar system, had begun their own exploration of this requirement. On Earth, She had been experimenting with a body-form closely appearing like our own human form – Neanderthal Man, as well as numerous other "false starts".

The Earth was not alone in this choice, the planetary consciousness that is Mars had also been developing a primary life-form along human lines. However, the Mars "humans" were a little more advanced than the ones the Earth had developed so when the Earth decided to begin again, She adopted the proto-human form from Mars. So no, it is not quite "Men are from Mars and Women are from Venus", but close. We know this Earth/Martian hybrid proto-human as "Cro-Magnon Man".

This is why Cro-Magnon Man appeared spontaneously across the whole planet 3.6 million years ago.

So what we have, from about 3.6 million years ago, is a basic human form, Cro-Magnon Man, as the basis for a being which the Earth hopes will develop into a form which will be capable of accommodating a full soul. This is the fundamental Question behind life on Earth – is it possible to build a fully physical being who has the whole of the soul contained *within* the body; this is part of the fundamental Question this Universe was Created to answer.

Following the solar system-wide disaster, the removal of four planets 3.9 m years ago, this is what the Earth began to explore.

Life develops in two stages, there is a primary act of creation and then, that which has been created is allowed to evolve by itself into the directions that it is able or chooses to go. So the process of creation and evolution go hand in hand – neither could happen without the other.

There is no point in creating something if it cannot evolve and something cannot evolve if it was not first created.

In this instance, as with most planetary life throughout the universe, it is the consciousness of the home planet that creates the forms of life and they are then given the opportunity to develop, to evolve, as they will.

This is how life on Earth works, the Earth decides what to create, She builds an energetic template (sometimes called the "etheric template"), a pattern of energies around which that form of life will grow, and the densities of energies available on Earth give it its physical substance.
This is how all life on Earth came into being and how they continue to exist. If the Earth changes Her mind, or feels that a particular form of life is not really viable, She removes the energetic template and the form of life gradually disappears off the planet.

How humans began life is slightly different in that the Earth adopted our energetic template from one developed on Mars, but the principle is still the same. Human development has occurred by our energetic template being modified and refined until we end up with our current body form of Homo Sapien Sapien.
But, it is not quite that simple, some modifications were made to our human form that made us a much greater being that we currently are. We might think that we are the pinnacle of human development, according scientific arrogance, whereas, in fact, we are considerably less than we once were.

To understand what the Akashic means by that, we have to travel back in time to about 98,000 years ago to a place we know as Lemuria.

There are many legends and stories about this place, most appear to be fantasy rather than truth. As far as the Akashic is concerned, Lemuria was an ice island just off the tip of South America. This island of ice was chosen for several reasons but the main one was that it was uninhabited and away from the other land-masses. The purpose of Lemuria was to study the development of human beings or, more correctly, to study why human beings were so slow in developing.

Those who did the studying were from one of the semi-physical races – those who originate from a star system we have designated NGC 584, this is just an astronomers cataloguing system number and has no significance beyond that. These beings do have a name for each other but the human voice box is incapable of pronouncing it, so we have to stick with NGC 584 or NGC for short.

Those who originate on NGC 584 are master geneticists. They hold the genetic records of every single form of life that has ever existed anywhere throughout this universe. Not only do they carry these records, but are capable of re-building any of these life-forms anywhere they are required.

These beings have worked with the Earth ever since the Earth wanted to develop life and several of the early experimental forms that appeared on Earth were brought here, and modified by the NGC, to suit the energy patterns that exist on Earth. Because of their history, the NGC were the perfect people to carry out the investigation that the Earth had asked for - to find out why Cro-Magnon Man was so slow in developing into a body form that could support the whole of a soul.

The answer, arrived at by the NGC, was not entirely conclusive and they recommended that some genetic acceleration be carried out to help these proto-humans to fulfil their potential. This proposal was considered and about 85,000 years ago a new research facility was established on an island in the Atlantic we know as Atlantis.

Atlantis was more of a continent than an island as it stretched from the west coast of Ireland, diagonally across the Atlantic Ocean as far as the Caribbean basin. Again, this particular continent was chosen as it was detached from all other land masses because if anything went wrong with the experimental work that was proposed to happen on Atlantis, no other forms of life would be affected.

You have to remember that we live in a universe where every single soul has absolute freedom of choice to choose their actions. Nobody can act in such a way as to remove freedom of choice (one exception to this rule did occur and that story is covered in my other books). In this way, every single Cro-Magnon Man (and woman) was asked if they wanted to take part in the type of work that was proposed to be carried out. Although not very developed, they were able to understand what was being asked of them. Some of the population of Atlantis said that they did want to be a part of what was going on whilst others said they did not. Those who did not want to be a part of what was happening were moved to another part of the planet, of their choosing, and were left to develop as they chose.

If nobody had wanted to be a part of this experiment, the experiment would not have occurred and Cro-Magnon Man would have been allowed to develop as it would, without any kind of outside interference. This is freedom of choice in action. Those who remained on Atlantis underwent a form of genetic acceleration.

Those who originate on NGC 584 do not have any kind of agenda. As far as they are concerned, they have developed skills which they freely offer to the rest of the Universe without limit or without charge. They do what they do because they are masters at it and they enjoy what they do, there is no other reason behind their

41

actions. They are not like our current human geneticists who, apart from not actually knowing what they are doing, have all sorts of hidden agendas behind their work (see *Project Human Extinction*). But for now, let us return to Atlantis.

The problem with Cro-Magnon was that, like all animal life on Earth, they had a group soul. In other words they were not individual souls but a part of a mass soul to which they were all connected. At birth, they started to draw from this mass soul and became individuals. Some drew in more of this mass soul and so were more intelligent and more physically developed than others. But, either way, they were not individuals as we would understand the term but more like a flock or a herd.

Their DNA structures were also very crude, just sufficient to give an individual an identity. What was done was that their energetic templates were developed so that the body became more advanced and this created more DNA. At each readjustment of their energies, the more they advanced until they reached a point where they were able to break away from their soul group consciousness and become individuals with the capacity to take on their own souls.

In order to fulfil this potential, the next stage was for an individual soul to come to Earth and take on the physical body that had been developed. This was not body snatching but by developing a new energy template, it was possible for a soul to come to Earth, borrow the energy template and to build a physical body around the template – a process called adult birth. This is the true origin of the Adam and Eve story.

This process is also one which the Annunaki have stolen to add to their fantasy version of human development.

We all have deep seated memories of Atlantis and our genetic acceleration. What the Annunaki hoped to achieve with their version of our history was to make us believe that our currently very vague memories of our own genetic acceleration was in fact

42

carried out by the Annunaki to create the adamu and not decisions we made ourselves about our development and how that development was carried out.

With this adult birth process proven to work, more souls came from the Universe and a community of human beings began to develop on Atlantis.

Most of the souls who came to Earth to be a part of this new experiment were from the non-physical races, with some coming from the semi-physical races. The proportions at this stage were roughly three quarters were of the non-physical races and about one quarter from the semi-physical races.

This is how human life was developed on Atlantis and this is what the Earth considers to be a full human being – a whole soul within a physical body. There was not the division between the physical aspect of the soul and the higher aspect of the soul as we currently experience life, but the whole of the soul within the physical body.

Our current state of being, the body containing the physical self with an attached, but not integrated, higher self, the Earth considers to be sub-human.

Life on Atlantis

I will try to paint a picture of life on Atlantis although it is not so easy to do as we do not have the vocabulary to explain it fully, but I will try my best.

The Earth's axis was vertical, not tilted as it is now, so the climate was very settled. Day time temperatures were in the low thirties centigrade and it did not rain very often. When it did rain, it was gentle and refreshing. Carbon dioxide levels were higher than present. This higher level of carbon dioxide actually helps the brain to function more efficiently, something which was needed to help human development.

The current change in carbon dioxide levels is actually a natural process as we approach a time when we will be able to live as we once did on Atlantis. Current carbon dioxide levels are rising as part of a natural process brought about by the Earth and have nothing to do with human activities – I'll come back to this later.

As far as humans were concerned, we were very much in advance of how we are now. We did not speak to each other but communicated psychically, this meant that there were no limits to our ability to communicate fully so there were never any misunderstandings.

If we wished to travel anywhere, we projected our thoughts to where we wished to be, a little like remote viewing, and then carried the body along with the thought – a process called translocation. Or by using this same process, we could be in two places at once – bi-location.

Our bodies were very much less dense than they are now so we needed very little in the way of solid food – generally just some fruit or if we needed a little more protein, we ate sea weeds which we synthesised for our needs.

We could communicate with all living things and so wild animals were never a threat, we just lived in total harmony with everyone and every thing. This is how human life should be lived, a true "Garden of Eden".

This is a very long story and I have tried to tell it as best I can in my previous books so, to cut a long story short, things began to go wrong and, at the time, we could not work out why they had gone wrong. The problem was that we began to lose some of our "higher" functions, especially our abilities to translocate and the finer aspects of our psychic communications. Just as we began to investigate the root cause of these problems, another situation occurred which could have had devastating affects on the life of the whole planet. This potential disaster situation is too long to go into here but is explained in my previous books.

The ultimate outcome of these events was that we eventually, collectively, decided to destroy the continent. This we achieved psychically by opening up the mid-Atlantic fault line, surrounded the continent in volcanoes and deliberately sinking Atlantis into the Earth's molten core. This destruction occurring about 65,000 years ago. This is why no physical evidence for the existence of Atlantis remains, all was deliberately destroyed by sinking it into the magma.

Sinking the continent had far reaching and potentially devastating effects on the planet. The planet's axis tilted altering the climate. Many earthquakes and volcanoes were triggered together with massive tsunamis, creating huge areas of flooding and most of the life on Earth was threatened with extinction. The planet also shrank in size to about ten percent smaller than She is now.

*This is the real origin of the Biblical story of the flood and it occurred 65,000 years ago and **not** 13,000 years ago.*

As far as the human population was concerned, those who were souls from the non-physical races returned to their home worlds whilst most of those who were from the semi-physical races stayed to help re-build the Earth and its life. This re-building work took over 40,000 years to complete and the Earth was fully ready to begin again about 20,000 years ago.

Life After Atlantis

When we returned, by "we" I mean all of the souls who had chosen to be a part of this new experiment of being human, we were as we had been on Atlantis; the whole soul within the body and, also as on Atlantis, we did not have any children.

A human being is defined as a physical body which contains the whole soul and we had not fully worked out a mechanism for dividing the soul into separate parts so that children could be born.

When a child is conceived, the foetus does not contain any consciousness. The physical act of sperm meeting egg generates a chain reaction of cell production which makes use of the DNA of both parents. At about 16 days (598 cell divisions) into the pregnancy, the soul of the child begins to make contact with the foetus and starts to imprint its own DNA onto the developing cells. After about sixteen weeks the child's consciousness begins to enter the foetus but only very slowly. By the time of birth, the newly emerged child contains about one quarter of the soul's energies that are to make up the level of consciousness within the physical body for this lifetime. Following birth, the remainder of the soul's physical aspect slowly enters the body until the final "piece" enters at puberty. We had not worked out this process at the time of Atlantis.

So, when we returned to Earth 20,000 years ago, our method of arrival was through adult birth. In the end, we thought sex looked like it had interesting possibilities and so we did eventually work out how to have children, around about 16,000 years ago.

On our return to Earth, instead of choosing a separate continent, as we had with Atlantis, we decided to build new "colonies" in six separate locations dotted around the planet. These were Northern Europe (Britain, Ireland and northern France); northern South America (Mexico, Guatemala and Belize); Sumeria (Southern

Turkey, parts of Syria and Iran and Iraq); Egypt; Tibet; and Southern Greece.

Each of these six groups took on a particular role in terms of investigating what had gone wrong on Atlantis - why did we have the kinds of problems that led to our loss of higher psychic functions?

The one region which took something of a lead role in these investigations was the one in Southern Sumeria – this is the region around the Tigris and Euphrates rivers – modern-day Iran and Iraq.

This region was important as it took on a role of what could be described as "scientific" in that it investigated every single aspect of life and how it functioned within the Earth's energy fields. We know about this region as it developed telescopes, microscopes, healing by herbs, aromatherapy, surgery and microsurgery and what we would call technological ways of investigating.

This is the region of Sumeria that the Annunaki targeted by travelling back in time to 5,000 years ago.

As happened on Atlantis, and as we had anticipated, we began to lose many of our higher aspects of full consciousness. We began to lose many of the higher brain functions such as the ability to translocate and bi-locate and even our abilities to communicate psychically became difficult.

In order to remedy these losses, 18,000 years ago we built the Egyptian and South American pyramids and the pyramids in many other regions of the world.

These pyramids were never intended to be used as tombs and, in fact, never were. Archaeologists have never found bodies in any of the pyramids apart from one or two burials that took place a long time after the pyramids were built and even these burials were not in any of the main chambers but in chambers excavated specially for the later burial.

48

The pyramids were designed and built to be psychic enhancers. In other words, as we began to lose our psychic capabilities, we entered the main chambers of the pyramids and, using sound sequences, we triggered very powerful standing-wave energy patterns within the pyramid itself. These standing-wave energies were powerful enough to re-merge the soul back into the body and our full psychic potential was restored.

In order to help us understand and remember how to use the pyramids, some people took on the role of "teachers" to help guide those who had lost these higher faculties to restore them. These teachers learned all of the sound sequences necessary to trigger the pyramids' energies and they became what could be considered the first form of "priesthood". The sound sequences are also the true "Keys of Enoch".

But, even with these teachers, we still lost our higher brain functions. Most people did not mind too much as they still had abilities far beyond anything we have now, but, a few did decide to maintain all of their potential and these later developed into the Pharaoh.

This situation also gave rise to the beginnings of members of a society having a greater knowledge than the remainder – the beginnings of secret societies.

Eventually, we worked out why we were losing our higher brain functions – the Earth, in order to bring about physical life, generated an energy signal of 7.56 cycles per second (7.56 Hz). In other words, to be physical, we needed to slow the energy frequencies of the soul to match the Earth's own lowest frequency and this 7.56 cycles per second was too low a frequency to maintain all of the soul within the body for any length of time. The problem was that no one could work out what the correct frequency should be.

What we, collectively, decided to do was to formulate a plan, a way in which we could learn how to be fully human again but, this time, being human in a way which allowed us to keep all of our soul's potential intact together with all of our higher psychic abilities.

The Human Plan

The Human Plan was this: We would divide the soul into two parts; the physical aspect and the higher aspect – the physical aspect being about one quarter of the total soul with the higher aspect being the remaining three quarters. In energy terms, the total soul is comprised of 50 dimensions, this division within the soul means that the physical aspect contained about twelve dimensions of soul energy – remember these 12 dimensions.

The physical aspect would live out a series of lifetimes learning everything that it was possible to learn about living a physical life on Earth – a process we know as reincarnation.

As we lived each lifetime, the knowledge we gained would be recorded, first by the higher aspect of the soul and then by the Akashic. This knowledge gathering process we know by the Sanskrit name of Karma. This is all that Karma originally meant – knowledge. The meaning has been misinterpreted and new interpretations have been attached to this word over the centuries but all it actually means is Knowledge.

Whilst the lower aspect was living out its chosen lifetime, our higher aspect would ensure that we kept on the straight and narrow path we had mapped out between lives, by communicating through the seven primary chakras – the chakras are actually aspects of the total soul within the physical body. This communication took the form of an illness. If we strayed from our chosen path, the energies of one, or more, chakras would become depleted, we would feel symptoms of illness and then we could regain our health by listening to the message our higher aspect was giving us and return to our path in life.

This is all that an illness is; a message from our higher self to tell us that we were not living our lives quite as we should and we needed to correct our behaviour.

Collectively, we all agreed to be a part of this plan and it was put into action 7,000 years ago. We gave ourselves a time limit of 7,000 years and this time limit runs out at the end of 2011.

This plan is known as The Human Plan and every single person who has lived on Earth since has been working within this plan.

This is the purpose of human life – to find out how we re-merge the whole soul back into the body and we, and the Earth, gave ourselves 7,000 years in order to achieve our aim.

So why 7,000 years? And why the end of 2011 running in to the end of 2012?

If you remember back to what we said earlier about all life within the solar system being destroyed 3.9 million years ago; the solar system has been effectively dead ever since. That is, apart from one planetary moon, there is no other life within our solar system whereas before 3.9 million years ago, every planet supported life.

Life in our solar system is an experiment to find out whether life at the kind of energy frequencies we call physical can exist – we are here to fulfil the Creator's wish, to answer the Creator's "Question".

With life on Earth, in the intervening time, proving to be so successful, the rest of the solar system has decided to come back to life. Since the end of the 1960's our Sun has been generating more and more energies within the heliosphere to allow the other planets to wake up.

To help in this new choice for life, we are also taking advantage of the energy patterns that are available from the centre of our galaxy – this is one of the main reasons for the end of 2012 being so important, this energy from the galactic centre will be at its peak. We decided to complete our own waking up process, the reintegration of the soul back into the body, at the end of 2011 to allow us to assist in the solar system-wide wake up.

So what does this mean for us individually?

First of all, we are not "Ascending" anywhere, the term Ascension was termed by the Annunaki to try to make us believe that in order to further evolve we must "Ascend" off the planet and go somewhere else. Remember that the Earth defines a human being as a physical body that contains the whole of the soul and this is the purpose of The Human Plan – to find a way in which we could achieve this again. So why would we need to go away from the Earth to achieve this?

To many people this may sound impossible but, there are currently (mid 2010) 4.5 million people on Earth who have already achieved full soul reintegration back into the body. The vast majority of these full human beings live in isolated communities in isolated regions of the planet so it is unlikely you will encounter them until you complete your own part of this reintegration process. Let's face it, if these reintegrated souls were in the western world, they would either be rounded up by the military and experimented on or they would be turned into a new religion; or both. If you did encounter one of these "new humans", they would place themselves behind psychic barriers in order that they would not be seen or discovered.

In fact, the first people to undergo the final stages of their soul reintegration did so on June 2nd 2003. There were two small groups, a total of 68 people, one in Europe and one in America. 24 of the 25 of the American group were immediately taken into custody by the military and have been experimented on ever since, two of whom have died because of these experiments. This group of 25 were aware that they had been under psychic observation for quite some time and so were fully aware of the fact that the moment they reintegrated they would be taken into a military base and be experimented on. This they volunteered to do with full knowledge of what they faced. They did this in order to satisfy the curiosity of the military in the hope that they would leave others alone. This sacrifice seems to have worked.

The Effects of the Annunaki Plan

Before we go on to look at how you can achieve this process of reintegration for yourself, we need to take a look at the implications of the Annunaki Plan and how it is being used to stop us from achieving our individual re-integrations.

The main tool used against us, you and me that is, is fear. By creating fear within the population you create control and by promoting the Annunaki version of human history, you also create confusion.

The basic structure of fear and confusion is this:

The Annunaki took over the Illuminati, when it was formed in 1776, and have been in control ever since. The first act of the Illuminati was to design and bring about the French Revolution in order to bring about a socialist state. When the French Revolution failed, the European monarchs became very wary of dealing with the Illuminati and, effectively, threw them out of Europe.

Having been ostracised in this way, the Illuminati moved their centre of operations to America and have controlled the political, monetary and military systems there ever since.

With America firmly under the control of the Illuminati, their next act was to finance and control the Russian Revolution; this was financed and engineered by American and British banks.

The extremely poor and virtually unknown Lenin was given passage to America and feted and groomed to become the leader of the Revolution. When the time was right, arms and money were supplied to bring the Russian Revolution about.

More recently, the Illuminati are in the process of trying to build a centrally controlled socialist Europe through the Lisbon treaty. This treaty wipes out the sovereignty of every EU country and will effectively remove free elections as all regional leaders, or Commissars, will be appointed by Brussels – this is happening under our very noses.

In order to bring about the plans of the Illuminati, they have created NGO's – Non-Governmental Organisations – such as The World Bank, World Health Organisation, World Trade Organisation, United Nations, Trilateral Commission, and many, many others to take total control of our health, finances and what we can or cannot eat.

The 'meltdown' of numerous banks and insurance companies during 2008 & 2009 were as a direct result of Illuminati actions as was the Trillions of pounds given by governments (tax payer's money), around the world, to bail out these companies.

To coordinate these governments and NGO's, the Illuminati created the Bilderberg Group. This is an organisation set up to pass Illuminati instructions on to government leaders, the heads of media corporations and the heads of trans-national businesses.

To work on a more personal level, the higher level (30th level and above) Freemasons were set up to pass on information and instructions to people like police chiefs and bank managers.

This does not mean that all Freemasons are complicit within this arrangement. Those Freemasons below the thirtieth level follow the Scottish Rites of Freemasonry and generally do not know much about the higher levels.

Those Freemasons, who are promoted to the thirtieth rank, and especially above, in America known as Shriners, follow the New Palladian Rites which begin to allow them access to the secrets of the Annunaki story and recognise Lucifer as the "God" of Freemasons and the Illuminati.

Lucifer is one of the roles and titles taken on by the Velon/Annunaki consciousness.

Control of Science

All of the organisations within this Velon/Annunaki/Illuminati hierarchy work together to control every aspect of our lives and to control our thoughts. For example: we have touched on official scientific versions of events with the false human history but, in addition to this, there are other fundamental untruths such as the

Big Bang – this did not occur and many cosmologists are now beginning to counter Big Bang Theory. This is to do with the distribution of background radiation throughout the Universe. If the Big Bang did occur, the distribution of radiation patterns could not be as they have been observed and measured.

Double Dark Theory (Cold Dark Matter and Cold Dark Energy) for the Universe does not work, despite many billions of pounds being spent on building particle accelerators in various countries over the past thirty years or so, most recently on the Swiss-French border.

These particle accelerators have been built in a vain attempt to find a sub-atomic particle known as a "Higgs Boson", or a "Higgs Field", depending on which quantum physicist you speak to. This particle is meant to convert energy into matter. The need for this arises as Cosmologists can only account for a small amount of the matter that should exist in the Universe to make gravity work.

Gravity does not exist, the Universe is held together by consciousness. We, and other life, are connected to Earth not by gravity but by compatible frequencies of soul energy – our individual souls connect in directly with the Earth's consciousness – this is what actually keeps us, and all other life, on the planet and stops us from drifting off into space. The same principle applies to the rest of the Universe; the Universe itself, as well as all galaxies and solar systems, are all held together by consciousness energies.

These Universe-wide consciousness energies have been measured by scientists as electro-magnetic frequencies. In other words, we live in an electro-magnetic Universe (consciousness energies) and not in a Universe held together by gravity. When the Universe, and our solar system, is viewed in this way, all of the anomalies that scientists cannot answer, or invent a new sub-atomic particle to explain, fade away and everything makes very simple sense.

Magnetic Pole Shift

As we undergo a change in our own levels of consciousness, so is the Earth. For example, the move of the magnetic pole towards the equator is not happening. What is happening is that the rotational axis is moving north – the Earth is returning to the vertical rotation we had at the time of Atlantis – the magnetic pole is not moving; it is its relationship to the rotational axis that is changing.

Much has been made of this supposed change in the magnetic pole in the press as a means of generating fear and disquiet by making us believe that the pole could "flip" and wipe out all electrical equipment with the biggest fear generating scenario of all – mobile phones would stop working!

International Terrorism

Another example would be the myth of world terrorist organisations such as Al-Qaeda. MI6, now known as the SIS, admitted that a "rogue" cell within their organisation planned, armed, recruited and trained those who carried out the London 7/7 bombings. This admission was made by an SIS spokesman live on the BBC 6 o'clock evening news and never reported anywhere again (I actually watched the news broadcast live).

All of the evidence shows very clearly that the Twin Tower demolition on 9/11 was carried out by American secret service operatives and not foreign terrorists. The evidence for this is overwhelming; it is just ignored and buried by the media.

The War on Iraq

Have you wondered why the west declared war on Iraq? It had nothing to do with getting rid of Saddam Hussein nor weapons of mass destruction nor anything to do with Iraqi oil, the world is awash in oil so it does not need the Iraq oil wells and in any case, so much uranium was dumped onto Iraq with DU (depleted uranium) weapons that the oil is radioactive. The real reason for declaring war on Iraq is because it is the region where modern life began – ancient Sumeria.

The real reason for attacking Iraq is to remove, to the west, any evidence supporting the Annunaki fantasy story and also to destroy any evidence that contradicts the Annunaki fantasy story. This is also the main reason for war-mongering against Iran; it was also part of ancient Sumeria.

Climate Change

Then there is man-made climate change. This is a total hoax designed specifically to create an extra carbon tax as a means of financing The New World Order. Global temperatures have been rising since 1850. This was the date of the last Thames winter fayre which could only take place because the Thames froze over, the temperature rise since is due to natural fluctuations in preparation for our completion of the Human Plan, as is the increase in carbon dioxide I talked about earlier. Global temperatures actually stopped rising in 1995, according to the Metrological Office and, since 2000 has shown a slight drop. However, sun activity is set to begin rising again so it looks as though we will see global temperatures beginning to rise as a result of this renewed activity in the near future.

To understand just how much of a hoax this is, we need to look at the Earth's climate over a period of several thousand years. All of the dates and figures quoted here are from the Metrological Office. Also, the way in which global temperatures are represented needs to be understood.

The planet has two poles, North and South, and the Equator. The Equator is obviously very hot whilst the two poles are very cold. Heat flows from the Equator and gradually becomes cooler the closer it approaches the poles. The global temperature figures given are the average temperatures for the whole of the planet's surface from pole to pole and are given in relation to zero. So a temperature of plus 1 degree C means the planet's average temperature was one degree Centigrade above freezing whilst a figure of minus 1 degree C means the planet's average temperature was one degree Centigrade below zero. Obviously, this is a very complex system and this is a very simplistic explanation and is given here to try to explain how the climate change propaganda manipulated the figures to give a very false impression.

If we go back several thousand years, we find that the average temperatures were very much higher than at present, around about plus 5 degrees C, this is reflected in the fact that herds of rhinoceros roamed southern Britain. If we look at about two thousand years ago, the average temperature was at least plus 3 degrees C as the Romans grew grape vines, producing a very drinkable red wine, along Hadrian's Wall on the Scottish borders. The temperatures then dropped a little, to about zero degrees C but then climbed again to produce the "Medieval Warm Period" where temperatures were about plus 2.5 degrees C. Around about the year 1300, temperatures began to drop, passing the zero point in 1480, eventually reaching minus 1.5 degrees C. The temperature began to rise again in about 1820, reaching zero degrees C in 1850.

This means that between 1480 and 1850 the average global temperature was below freezing. Scientifically, this period is known as the "Mini Ice Age".

This is why all of the temperature graphs used to make us believe that "man's activities" are to blame for "Global Warming" start at 1850, they totally ignore all of the natural temperature cycles that occurred before then where "man's activities" could not possibly have had any bearing on temperature change.

The "Mini Ice Age" had a devastating affect on human life. The British weather was so cold that it could snow at any time of the year with frequent snow showers being reported in July from the Midlands northwards. Population numbers dropped radically as it was not possible to grow enough food and diseases were rife. The most common cause of death was from the "Ague" (pronounced aagew) which was the common name for malaria. All sorts of other life-threatening illnesses were also rife because of malnutrition.

However, once the temperatures started to rise, population numbers grew, malnutrition ceased to be so much of a problem and the number of diseases dropped radically. For example, common causes of death in children under the age of 15 were scarlet fever, diphtheria, whooping cough and measles. In 1860 total deaths per year, from these diseases, were 6,200 for every one million children in Britain. By 1940 the number of deaths, from these illnesses had dropped to below 1,000 per million – a drop of ninety per cent. This also shows up the false claims by the medical profession that vaccinations and immunisation are the cause of better health.

It was the rise in temperatures and more food that reduced these deaths and not any other cause.

Since 1850, the temperature continued to rise until 1995 where it levelled out at plus 1.5 degrees C – a full one degree C lower than average temperatures during the "Medieval Warm Period", and since 2000, the average global temperature has begun to slowly drop.
It should also be noted that throughout all of these temperature fluctuations over these thousands of years, carbon dioxide levels have lagged behind the temperature increase.

*In other words, rises in carbon dioxide **follow** temperature rise and **do not cause** temperature rise.*

One of the main tools used to make us believe that Global Warming is caused by man's activities is the Oscar winning film called *"An Inconvenient Truth"* by Al Gore. In 2009, the British High Court made a ruling on this film based on 26 claims that the film contained. None of these 26 claims could be substantiated by British Government experts and so the High Court ruled the film amounted to propaganda. The High Court also ruled that the film should not be shown in schools unless "balancing material" was presented with it (the full High Court ruling is readily available on the Internet). It is also interesting to note that the film's maker, politician Al Gore, prior to the film's release set up, with business partners, a "bank" that trades in carbon futures. Al Gore, and his business partners, are now billionaires.

Population Increase

Along with climate change, we have the myth of a rising global population. Official government figures state that the world population is about 6.9 billion and rising. This is a lie. The main reason for this lie is so that the growth of GM crops is promoted in order to "feed the world". Apart from the fact that GM crops are increasingly failing and eating them is causing new diseases in both humans and animals, the real reason is again fear (see *"The Seeds of Destruction"* by F William Engdahl – see Bibliography).

So let us look at the real population figures.

Virtually every country has reported a population drop over at least the last ten years. Western countries are shutting schools due to lack of pupils, in other words, the birth rate is extremely low. The death rate is so high that governments are forcing people to work far beyond the age of sixty five.

Every western country is having to bring in migrant workers just to maintain the current workforce levels. Many eastern European countries are now virtually empty of people as the population has left to work in other countries.

Most third world countries have dropping populations due to famine, wars and mass vaccination programmes.

So how can we have a rising world population?

According to the Akashic, the world population peaked at 7.4 billion in 1996. Since then it has been rapidly falling to the point where in mid 2010 it was around 4 billion and it is continuing to drop.

The reason why people are starving in many countries is not too many mouths to feed but too much land has been given over to the growing of crops for bio-fuels, so much so that many countries cannot grow enough food to feed the people.

The list goes on. We have been fed fabrications and lies to make us more compliant and fearful. Fortunately, as we progress through our change of consciousness, these kinds of lies can be spotted much more easily and hence the rise in the number of people speaking out against these atrocities.

Actions Taken to Specifically Promote the Annunaki Plan

Let us start with the use of technology such as HAARP which stands for "High-energy Active Auroral Research Programme". The first HAARP station was built in Alaska but there are now several others dotted around the planet. The Military claim that it is not a military project but was set up for use by the military for "over the horizon" radar and communications. It might very well be used for these purposes but its two main uses are weather modification, mainly to cause droughts and famines but more recently, it has been used to flood the Earth with Extra Low Frequency waves.

These ELF waves are intended to slow down the Earth's rising frequencies (from 7.56 Hz to 3.5 KHz) as well as to slow down our own consciousness reintegration. These are very deliberate acts and have caused some disruption to our process of change.

UFO Disclosure

We are also likely to see, in the very near future, a general disclosure of the UFO contact information held by the United States. This massive cover up has been going on since 1947 and the Roswell crash. However, this will be a limited disclosure of evidence as it will be geared towards making us believe that the Annunaki are our makers and the "gods" of the Old Testament. This Annunaki disclosure will be linked in to the Human Genome Project, indicating that the "elite" carry Annunaki genes. This disclosure is also designed to destroy current religious beliefs.

Whilst there have been many sightings of UFO's, or NTV's as they are now officially called (Non-Terrestrial Vehicles), over many years, many of which are genuine, in more recent years, the vast majority of sightings of NTV's have been of secret military craft that have been built using technology copied from downed NTV's.

At the same time as these "human UFO's" are appearing, there is also the emergence of a new technology, namely hologram projectors.

This hologram technology has been developed over a number of years by the military and the film makers of Hollywood working together. This technology is now so advanced that holograms of NTV's have been projected into the sky.

The best examples of the use of this technology were the massive pyramid shaped NTV's that hung over the cities of Moscow and Peking in early 2010. I have searched the Akashic to try to find a race who have built pyramid shaped craft and there are none. The only source of this design of craft appears to be the Hollywood movie, and subsequent TV series, called "*Stargate*".

Not only is this technology capable of projecting massive moving craft, it has also been refined to project religious figures. The latest advances in this technology indicate that the holographic projections can be made to appear to speak. This gives a great potential for religious-type figures to appear in our skies and speak to the people gathered below.

No doubt 'Lord Sananda' and 'Lord Metatron' (see below) are eagerly awaiting the use of this technology to pass on the commands of the "Galactic Federation" and "Ashtar Command" to convince us that they do exist and are just waiting for the correct time before they evacuate the human population off the planet to a "5th Dimension" where we can all "Ascend"!

Black Holes and Wormholes

There have also been attempts to use HAARP technology to build "black holes" out of our solar system. The spiral that appeared over Norway in December 2009 was one such attempt as were the spirals that appeared over China and Japan in early 2010 – all HAARP generated.

All of these attempts failed to build a black hole, there is insufficient energy within our solar system for that to happen, but people believe that black holes were built and are interpreting these sky events as the arrival of the ships that are to take us off planet.

The same applies to the strange lights in the sky that many have taken to be "wormholes". In scientific terms, wormholes are back to back black holes.

Again, these so-called wormholes are produced by HAARP generating plasma streams in the upper atmosphere to make people believe that ships are arriving – the UFO that appears to emerge from the end of the plasma stream is just a plasma discharge as the stream is stopped.

Ships are not arriving; those who guard this solar system are ensuring that the Velon (Annunaki) cannot enter this solar system.

Of course, the HAARP technology could be being used to create these effects in our skies to make us **believe** that there are a number of NTV's arriving thereby furthering the aims of the Annunaki Plan - especially as there are no ships actually arriving.

"Channelled" Communications

The Annunaki and the Hathor have also been working very closely with those who "channel" information. These are psychics who are able to communicate with those souls who are no longer physical or those who are of non-physical origins; in other words, Extra Terrestrials.

Ever since Madam Blavatsky, who established the Theosophical Society, the Annunaki have been communicating through channels to provide us with massive amounts of disinformation designed to make us believe that they are here to help us in our process of soul reintegration.

Except, the way in which these channelled messages work is to try and make us believe that we are "Ascending". In other words, in order to fulfil our potential, we must "Ascend" off the planet to a "5th Dimension". In order to help us in this, the Annunaki have thousands of "cloaked" ships, within our solar system, ready to lift us off into space when we are ready – this mass evacuation is being coordinated by a group calling themselves "Ashtar Command" who are acting under the guidance of "The Galactic Federation". All of these messages and organisations are Velon (Annunaki) in origin. There are literally thousands of these kinds of messages from hundreds of organisations, individuals and "angels", all telling us that we must leave the Earth.

There are also a number of web sites appearing where an updated version of the Annunaki false history is being presented. This "new" version of history has become very detailed which is making it, to some people, more believable.
I can only reiterate that the history detailed within the Akashic, which is being brought to light by many people, is the true history of the Earth. This is borne out by numerous esoteric writings that have been in existence for thousands of years.

To give you one example of how those who channel can be misled. I received an email from someone who has been channelling "automatic writing" for many years, the channel has always assumed that the source of these messages was an "Angel". Having read the *Project Human Extinction* book, the channel decided to challenge their source. The source was very reluctant to reveal its true origin but, eventually, the source admitted that it was Velon.

My research shows that over 90 per cent of all channelled messages, over the last 50 years, are of Velon origin.

If you are approached by a source who wishes to channel through you, you must always check who that source is as it is easy to be misled, especially if you are inexperienced in these kinds of communications.

As a note about our "Ascending to a 5th Dimension". Having spent the last thirty years working with and exploring the energy patterns contained within the body, I have found that our bodies contain a huge range of energy frequencies. I said earlier that when we set the Human Plan into action, we divided the soul into two aspects, the higher and the physical with the physical aspect containing 12 dimensions. Dimensions are energy markers – no more than that, a little like the frequency markers on a radio dial. In these terms, the 5th dimension actually relates to the energy patterns within the physical body at about navel level. I am sure that we would all agree that "ascending" to your navel is not a step forwards in human evolution!

The Return of the "Christ Consciousness"

One of the most persistent of the individuals who is the source of a great deal of channelled writings calls himself Sananda. This name, Sananda, is claimed by the Velon to mean "the Ascended Christ" – the return of the "Christ Consciousness". Many, many people have fallen for this ploy as they see it as the "Second Coming" of Jesus, as predicted in the New Testament.

This ploy has led many people, particularly those of the Christian faith, to delay their own reintegration until "the Christ Consciousness" has returned. This is exactly what the Velon (Annunaki) want. They want people to delay their completion, they want people to be confused and want someone to step in and "Save" them; it is in this way that the Velon expand their control and remove peoples' freedom to choose their own path.

It is also interesting that this character has begun to call himself "Lord Sananda" who, along with his fellow "Lord", "Lord Metatron", are here to save us all. One question: - if these are beings that have "Ascended" to perfection, as they claim, why would they have an ego that requires the title "Lord"?

The Process of Completion

Despite all of these efforts to mislead and to stop us, we are changing, we are moving forwards and we are on time, we just need to understand that we are being manipulated. Once we understand that, we can let these fears go and get on with the things we need to do.

Firstly, do not, repeat do not become involved with mass meditations that ask for help in helping the Planet or meditations that claim to be changing planetary energies in any form, whether that is activating crystals or taking over energy points like Silbury Hill.

These types of meditations were designed to give the Annunaki control over these energies. Fortunately, those who act as guardians of the planet interceded and stopped the Annunaki's plans.

If you feel as though you have been requested to build a "portal", resist the urge to go out and so do. The Annunaki have been denied access to our solar system and the request for portals to be built was an attempt by the Annunaki to by-pass the solar system's and the Earth's defences.

As we undergo our process of change, so does the Earth. The Earth knows what She is doing and, more importantly, what needs to be done. If She has not already done so, all of the actions the Earth needs to undertake are in hand or underway and, for the time being, She does not need human intervention.

What we need to be doing is to bring ourselves to the point where we can all complete our soul reintegration and bring our individual actions and explorations within The Human Plan to its proper and final conclusion.

The best and only way, to help the planet and to help ourselves is to ignore all of these things. Yes, politicians and governments are trying to curtail our freedoms and are building many prison-like buildings where those who protest against the system will be held indefinitely without charge – this new legislation is already in place in all western countries, so mass demonstrations on the streets are just going to get you locked up.

The best way of defeating the plans of the Annunaki, and those governments and organisations that have already been enslaved by them, is to look to yourself and sort out any outstanding problems there are in your own life.

What do I mean by this?

Each individual is a soul who has built for itself a body. We are not a body with a soul but a soul who has chosen to live lifetimes on Earth and in so doing, the soul has built the bodies we inhabit. But, most of the soul has not been able to enter into the body because the energies of the planet were too low to sustain the total soul within the body. The Earth has done her bit – She changed her base-note energy frequencies from the original 7.56 cycles per second to 3,500 cycles per second (3.5 KHz); this She did on the 30th of May 2000. This is why everything feels as though it has accelerated since 2000; the Earth's energy frequencies have undergone a huge shift. What we need to do is to match the Earth's efforts and raise our own frequencies.

So how do we achieve this?

Firstly, **DO NOT PANIC**. Time might appear to be short but it is never too late and the processes we need to undergo are very simple and straightforward. Humans always have a tendency to try to make things complicated when, more often than not, the simple answer is the best and the most straightforward way of achieving what we need to achieve.

What we need to remember is that every single one of us, alive on this Earth at this time, chose to be born specifically to be a part of this process and period of change. This was a deliberate choice and is no accident. Everything we need to do is already in place, we planned our lives that way, and so we only need to take a few necessary steps to bring about our own completions.

First and foremost we need to make a decision. Do we wish to complete our part of the Human Plan or not? Nobody is standing in judgement here, only our full selves – the physical self and the Higher Self.

Once we make this decision, we need to make a very clear and sincere statement of intent to ourselves and to our Higher Self. This is also done quite simply – we just need to find a quiet time in our day, sit down quietly and say to yourself – "I sincerely wish to undergo this process of soul reintegration, please help me to achieve this by helping me to understand what further steps I need to take". If this statement is sincerely made, your Higher Self will do all that it can to help bring this change about. What we then need to do is to listen to the prompts our Higher Self makes. We have to pay attention to everything that happens in our life and resolve whatever it is that arises as it arises. The time where we can ignore the events of our lives and hope that we can deal with them at a future date is now long past.

We must deal with everything as it arises and we also need to clear out things from our past that we have not resolved. The reason for this is that we need to start making room in our bodies for the rest of the soul to download into.

Most of us are filled with unexpressed and unresolved emotions and all of this emotional debris takes up a huge amount of room, so we need to get this rubbish out. Most of the stored emotions stem from our not expressing ourselves fully; disputes with our boss, the neighbour, granny, our parents, brothers and sisters, children, whoever. Everyone we share our lives with has an emotional impact on us and unless we deal with these kinds of situations honestly, we end up storing all of the emotions we did not express.

Say you really felt like screaming and shouting at your boss, or whoever, and all you did was to mutter under your breath, all the screaming and shouting you didn't do becomes stored within the body.

The best way of emptying this debris out is to discuss it with the person who caused you problems. If that is not possible, you can write to them. This is writing in a particular way which sounds like it shouldn't work until you try it, you will be surprised at just how much emotional junk you are carrying around and how much can be cleared by using this method.

The "Giveaway"

What you do is to start with an old sheet of newspaper. Using a pencil, write to a person or situation that comes to mind, just write all over the newsprint. It does not matter what kind of language you use to express yourself, just as long as what you are saying reflects the feelings you are holding on to about that person or situation.

Once you have finished a piece, just rip it up and get rid of it.

Do not read it back; that is very important, do not read it back.

This is the reason for using a pencil on newspaper - you are bound to be tempted to read it but you can't read pencil on newspaper. If you read it back, you are just taking all of the emotions back into your body and you will have to start again.

You will know you have cleared a situation when you can think back on it and not feel any emotion attached to the situation. If you still feel emotions connected to that person or situation, you will need to do more writing.

Changes Within the Body's Energies

The main indicator of how we are changing is with the chakras. The chakras are aspects of the total soul within the physical body and are the means by which the higher aspects of the soul communicates to us.

As we begin to clear ourselves of our emotional debris, the chakras begin to change colour. We are used to the chakras being the rainbow colours; red, orange, yellow, green, blue, indigo and violet. Since May 30th 2000, nobody on the planet has these colours any longer. When the Earth changed her base-note frequency, the chakras almost automatically changed colour. Colour is only a product of frequency; if the frequency changes, so must the colour.

Put another way, if the frequencies of the body increase, it is impossible for the colours of the chakras to remain the same.

Most people now have colours which are spiralling golds, copper golds, blues, green, violet but mainly transparent. By transparent I mean pure energy that looks like the kind of heat-haze shimmer you get on hot summer days.

As you work through the process of clearing out your emotional debris, the chakras change again to total transparency. In other words all of the chakras lose their colours and they become the transparent heat haze shimmer of pure soul energy.

The next stage is where the chakras disappear altogether. What this means is that the spine becomes a smooth column of energy from the crown of the head to the base of the spine without specific chakras.

As someone who has worked as a healer and psychic surgeon for the past thirty years, I can see the energies within the body and believe me, this is what the body's energies are doing.

Once you have reached the point where you no longer have any defined chakras, that is as far as you can go until your higher self decides to complete the reintegration process.

The reintegration of the soul back into the body will happen no later than the end of 2012 (21/12/12).

Once we have completed this process of reintegration, we will have all of the knowledge and all of the abilities we need to remove the Annunaki and to clean up global pollution and all the other bad things we have done to this amazing planet and there will be no need to move to "Pandora".

Only you can choose to undergo this body and soul reintegration, nobody will, or can, decide for you. This is your choice, your soul and your life – don't be left behind.

Bibliography

Zecharia Sitchin:
The 12th Planet; The Stairway to Heaven; The Wars of Gods and Men; The Lost Realms; When Time Began; The Cosmic Code; Genesis Revisited; Divine Encounters.
Avon Books, New York 1976 to 1990
The Lost Book of Enki
Bear & Co 2002

Michael A Cremo & Richard L Thompson:
Forbidden Archaeology
Bhaktivedanta Book Publishing Inc, India 2005

Dr Steven Greer
Hidden Truth Forbidden Knowledge
Crossing Point, Virginia USA 2006

F William Engdahl
Seeds of Destruction
Global Research, Montreal, Canada 2007

Chris Thomas:
The Journey Home; The Fool's First Steps; Planet Earth - The Universe's Experiment; The Universal Soul; The Human Soul.
Capall Bann Publishing, Somerset 1998 to 2007

Chris Thomas with Dave Morgan:
Project Human Extinction - The Ultimate Conspiracy
Capall Bann Publishing, Somerset 2009

Chris Thomas & Diane Baker
Everything You Always Wanted to Know About Your Body But, So Far Nobody's Been Able to Tell You; The Sequel to Everything; The Healing Book.
Capall Bann Publishing, Somerset 1999 to 2003

Books by Chris Thomas

Books About Human History & Earth Mysteries

The Journey Home

We are Human

We bring together our inherent spiritual natures and dense physical bodies and try to make them fit. All of the difficulties that we have experienced through all of our many lifetimes have led us to create and perpetuate myths and mysteries that have only served to alienate and confuse us to a point where we have forgotten our true natures.

As we begin a new phase of human history and development, a new understanding is emerging which begins to break away from those who would keep our true place in the universe secret.

This book attempts to cut through the half truths and mysticism and put our history and state of being into plain language. Many of the answers to our age-old questions have been available since mankind appeared on Earth but, over the centuries, they have become hidden by personal interests and clouded by repetition and dogma.

104 pages paperback   ISBN 186163041-7   UK price: £7.95
Published by Capall Bann   www.capallbann.co.uk

The Fool's First Steps

It is the beginning of the twenty first century and we have walked a long and tortuous path to arrive at this time.

We have arrived, but for the moment, we are not sure where our journeying has brought us. Our arrival on new-old shores has, temporarily, made us lost.

As with the Fool of the Tarot cards, we have travelled full circle and are poised to start afresh.

This book takes the first few steps into a new understanding of many of the world's mysteries and begins to look outwards to other life on other worlds and how they have helped to shape our past and present.

We are not a body that has a soul but a soul, an immense eternal consciousness, which has built for itself a body.

We are starting to bring the body and the soul into an integrated one and realise that we are everything that we ever dreamed we are and considerably more.

178 pages paperback   ISBN 186163072-7   UK price: £9.95
Published by Capall Bann   www.capallbann.co.uk

Planet Earth - The Universe's Experiment

Who are we? Where do we come from? What is our purpose and why did it go so wrong?

Humans are not of the Earth but have arrived on this planet to explore. On our joyous arrival we encountered the spirits of the land – the Sidhé and the Faerie. As we became more human, we began to lose our memories of our origins and the knowledge of our true purpose and potential.

As we approach the completion of our climb back to reality, we are awakening to the ghosts of this knowledge.

Lemuria, Atlantis, the thirteen races have all played their part in "The Human Plan", all are now working to assist us to our chosen goal – full consciousness. But, time is short and unless we complete our journey soon, the Earth will be lost to us.

Virtually all of our experience and history is at odds with the scientific versions of our past, only the Akashic tells the real history. What is told here is the Akashic's story.

202 pages paperback   ISBN 186163 224 X   UK price: £11.95
Published by Capall Bann   www.capallbann.co.uk

The Universal Soul

Curiosity, this is how life begins.

A curiosity along the lines of "What If?" Together with the energy potential to imbue a lifeless void with the souls who are to explore the "what if" on behalf of the one who asked the question.

Our Universe explores the "what if "of freedom of choice. Every soul that exists within this Universe has the right to choose their own actions, their own directions. All choose freely without limitations.

The exploration of the physical has led to the existence of Earth and all of the life that our Earth supports – a miracle of creation and evolution.

There have been many trials and tribulations throughout our Universe and some of these events have brought the whole "thought" to a point of near destruction. One thing has sustained this Universe above all else – the Earth must be protected at virtually any cost.

With humanity finally finding the answers to a question we asked ourselves 20,000 years ago, we are entering a new phase of existence and this process has repercussions on the Universal whole.

192 pages paperback   ISBN 186163 273-8   UK price: £12.95
Published by Capall Bann   www.capallbann.co.uk

The Human Soul - Universal Soul 2

We live in troubled times which do not appear to be improving.

All of the promises of forward movement for the human race moving towards our completion appear to have ground to a halt. Not only halted but racing backwards to a point of self-destruction.

Our current state pushes us to look for answers, often without fully knowing what the questions are. But, the places we have traditionally looked towards to providing these answers are increasingly failing to give satisfaction.

The purpose of this book is to show why we are failing in our search for the truth. It also fully updates the problems generated by the race we know as the Velon under their more commonly known names of Hathor and Annunaki – their true story is not as they would have us believe.

By investigating these answers, both through the Akashic and published material, it is hoped to give enough information so that by gaining that knowledge and understanding, it will help you to take back your own power and achieve the longed for soul reintegration.

245 pages paperback   ISBN 1-86163-299-1   UK price: £13.95
Published by Capall Bann   www.capallbann.co.uk

Project Human Extinction - The Ultimate Conspiracy
By Chris Thomas with Dave Morgan

This is a book about power. The power to control the money supply, the power to control governments, the power to control multi-national business, the power to control the media, and above all, the power to prevent the identity of those in power from becoming known.

The ability to wield this power has become known as "The Conspiracy". This conspiracy has been at work for nearly 250 years and yet most are not even aware that it exists.

What this book does is to unlock the key secrets of the conspiracy and to identify the key players and the forces at work behind this power-base.

Many will find the findings shocking whilst others will have already arrived at a similar conclusion for themselves.

Whatever you thought was going on in the world is almost certainly wrong. This book can help you to understand why you have been so powerless for so long.

390 pages paperback   ISBN 1-86163-312-2   UK price: £16.95
Published by Capall Bann   www.capallbann.co.uk

Books About Healing by
Chris Thomas & Diane Baker

Everything You Always Wanted to Know About Your Body But, So Far, Nobody's Been Able To Tell You

Have you ever wondered why some people become ill and not others?

Do you know how the body really works?

Why do diets rarely work?

Is there an alternative approach to treating illness instead of prescriptive drugs?

This book leads you through the body, organ by organ, system by system in simple language and clear illustrations.

It relates each organ to its associated chakra and explains how our day to day lives have an influence on our health.

It also takes a look at how illnesses are brought about by past life traumas.

It is a very comprehensive look at the body and illness and deals with illness at a root cause level. The second half of this book also contains a comprehensive guide to many alternative treatments for all symptoms of ill health.

456 pages paperback   ISBN 186163098-0   UK price: £17.95
Published by Capall Bann   www.capallbann.co.uk

The Sequel to Everything – The Case Histories

Although this is a sequel, it can be read independently as it explores how the body really functions by using genuine case histories taken from the authors' "psychic surgery" clients.

Forty six case histories are discussed to illustrate how the body is a function of, and directly controlled by, the soul.

Symptoms of illness arise because we have taken a step away from our soul's purpose. This book helps to bring back full health and accelerate full consciousness integration by helping you to understand the messages from the soul through the body.

This book further explores how past life choices can have a profound affect on our health in this lifetime, travelling as far back as Atlantis and beyond.

There is also a section exploring food additives and chemical toxicity.

202 pages paperback   ISBN 186163 1375   UK price: £11.95
Published by Capall Bann   www.capallbann.co.uk

The Healing Book

We are all Healers.

All that we need to do is to stop telling ourselves that we are not.

This book is for those who wish to heal. It starts at the beginning of the healing process with simple, easily followed exercises which can begin to unlock the healing potential which is inherent in all of us.

These methods apply equally to humans and to animals.

If you do not have any experience of giving healing, but would like to learn, this book can set you on that path.

If you already work as a healer and would like to explore your greater potential, this book is also for you.

The first half of this book is about learning to heal from the beginning. The second half begins to explore some of the energy manipulation techniques used by the authors in their daily practise as "psychic surgeons".

132 pages paperback   ISBN 186163053-0   UK price: £8.95
Published by Capall Bann   www.capallbann.co.uk

To order **signed** or further copies of this book,

The Annunaki Plan? or The Human Plan?

Please write to:

Fortynine Publishers
PO Box 49
Llandysul
SA44 4YU
Please include your email address

Costs UK: £6.50 per book postage and packing free

Rest of EU: £6.50 per book plus postage and packing of £2 per address plus £1 per book (UK currency only)
Rest of the World: £6.50 per book plus postage and packing of £3 per address plus £1 per book (UK currency only)

Cheques or Postal Orders only and made payable to Chris Thomas

Cards NOT accepted at the above address

Note: We can only accept cheques in pounds sterling drawn on a British Bank

Please allow 14 days for delivery

This Book is also available from Cygnus Books (cards accepted)

www.cygnus-books.co.uk